"RATTY

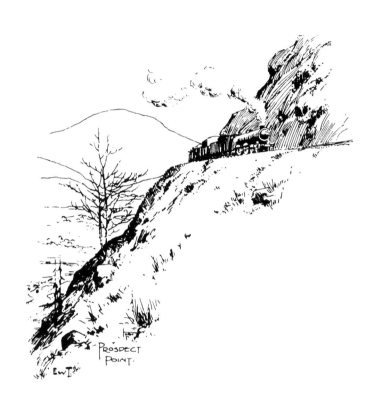

PROSPECT
POINT.

A HISTORY
OF THE RAVENGLASS
AND ESKDALE RAILWAY

By W. McGowan Gradon, B.A.

SECOND, REVISED EDITION
PLATEWAY PRESS

" RATTY "

A History of the Ravenglass and Eskdale Railway
W. McGowan Gradon, B.A.

First edition, 1947

This second, revised edition, 1997
ISBN 1 871980 30 5

Front cover illustration:
Locomotive Publishing Co., Ltd., postcard captioned –
"Eskdale Railway. The Eskdale Express approaching Bridge where
main road crosses the Railway. This is one of the many picturesque
spots on this unique little Railway."
Collection: A. Neale.

Rear cover illustration:
Lochinvar postcard with no caption other than that reproduced –
"Boot Express, Eskdale, Smallest Railway in England."
Collection: K. Taylorson.

Book Design: Roy C. Link

Published and distributed by:
PLATEWAY PRESS
Taverner House, Harling Road
East Harling, Norfolk NR16 2QR

CONTENTS

NOTES ON THIS EDITION

In preparing this new revised edition of W. McGowan Gradon's classic history of the Ravenglass & Eskdale Railway the original text has been left almost entirely as written. Where necessary any factual corrections have been indicated by an appropriate footnote. Any typographic errors have been corrected, as have mis-spellings of locomotive names etc. However, the opportunity has been taken to include a completely different selection of illustrations. These include some views taken in the 1950's as it is felt that the railway changed so little from the time of the First edition (1947) to the preservationist's takeover in 1960 as to justify this.

A. Neale, Plateway Press, 1997

DEDICATION

In memory of the late BRIAN HILTON,
a good friend of both 'RATTY'
and Plateway Press,
who would have been delighted to see both his photographs
and examples from his postcard collection
appear in print for the pleasure of all.

SOURCES OF ILLUSTRATIONS

The pictures used to illustrate this revised, second edition of 'RATTY' have all come from the personal collections of Keith Taylorson and Andrew Neale. Wherever possible we have credited the photographer or postcard publisher, only attributing those from sources unknown to our own collections. We will be pleased to hear from anyone who can definitely attribute any of the anonymous illustrations so that an appropriate note of correction can be made in any future edition.

AUTHOR'S PREFACE TO FIRST EDITION

A MONG railway enthusiasts of all ages the fascination of narrow gauge railways occupies prominent place. Although there are only a small number in active operation today in Britain, there are few with a more interesting history than the Ravenglass and Eskdale Railway, always affectionately referred to by the dalesfolk of this Western Lakeland beauty spot as "Ratty." Starting in comparative obscurity as a purely mineral carrying line (3 ft. gauge) over 60 years ago, it lay derelict for some time before re-opening as a 1 ft. 3 ins. gauge railway in 1915. Soon its fame as "the smallest railway in the world" spread over the whole country. Another concern lays claim to that title today and during the past ten years "Ratty" has lost much of the scale model character which it possessed in its earlier days as a "model" railway. Nevertheless the R. & E.R. is still going strong, carrying thousands of passengers up and down the lovely Eskdale valley in the tourist season and many thousand tons of red granite from Beckfoot Quarry all the year round.

In compiling this little history I am indebted to the following people, who have supplemented my own knowledge of "Ratty," particularly concerning the old 3 ft. gauge line: Miss M. C. Fair, Mr. H. Woodley, Mr. P. A. LeNeve Foster, and last, but by no means least, Mr. Harry Hilton, the present General Manager of the R.& E.R. Mr. Hilton I have known since I was in "short pants" and he has been a veritable mine of information upon which I have drawn to the full.

Except where indicated all photographs are the work of Miss M. C. Fair and permission to reproduce them is gratefully acknowledged. The title page and line drawings are all the work of my old friend and colleague, Sydney Buckley.

W. McGowan Gradon, B.A.   Altrincham, 1947

PREFACE TO SECOND EDITION

W hen the first edition of this book appeared in 1947 the R.& E.R. was not just a tourist attraction but still carrying substantial quantities of local granite. Beckfoot Quarry closed in 1953 after which the railway was maintained purely for passengers until its sale to the preservationists in September 1960. Since then it has gone from strength to strength with new locomotives and stock and substantial rebuilding of the structures and permanent way to make it one of Britain's premier 15 in. gauge railways.

The original edition of 'RATTY' has been a much sought after out of print work for many years so that, hopefully, this new edition will meet a real need. In preparing it I have received considerable help from Keith Taylorson and Roy C. Link, who is responsible for the layout and design. Our grateful thanks are due to the Ravenglass & Eskdale Railway Preservation Society for permission to reprint the work.

Andrew Neale   Leeds, 1997

CHAPTER ONE
"OWD RATTY," 1875-1912

The second 3 ft. gauge 0-6-0T NAB GILL (Manning Wardle 629 of 1876) poses with its crew at Boot circa 1900. It was withdrawn needing repairs around 1905, leaving its older sister DEVON to work all traffic for the last few years of the original railway.
Photograph: Collection A. Neale.

IN common with its bigger brothers in West Cumberland, the Furness and the Whitehaven, Cleator and Egremont Railways, The Ravenglass and Eskdale Railway owed its existence to haematite iron ore. Although the main deposits lay some miles to the North (from Egremont to Lamplugh) and again to the south-west at Millom, small deposits of haematite had been proved in veins on the fells on either side of the little village of Boot near the head of the Eskdale Valley. Early in the 1870's these deposits were exploited by the Whitehaven Mining Company and a number of trial drifts were opened up. In the meantime some easy method of transporting the ore down to the Furness Railway from the comparative inaccessibility of the upper Eskdale valley was required. A light railway connecting Ravenglass with Boot was the obvious answer, and powers were obtained by the Whitehaven Mining Company to construct such a line, to a gauge of 3 ft., in 1873. Included in the Act were powers to construct a branch from Ravenglass station "to the seashore" at the latter village. This was, of course, never built, since Ravenglass "harbour," once quite a busy little port, had been silted up for years and is today merely a portion of the tidal estuary of the rivers Irt and Mite. The promoters may, however, have had dreams of the ore deposits in Eskdale proving so vast and remunerative that a harbour might eventually be built at Ravenglass from which haematite could be shipped.

Seven miles in length, the Ravenglass and Eskdale Railway was laid with light flat-bottomed Vignoles rails. It was opened for mineral traffic on May 24th, 1875. The authorised capital of

Another view of a 3 ft. train at Boot terminus. Note the run round loop with short loading siding.
Postcard: Collection A. Neale.

the Company was £36,000 in £10 shares, of which £24,000 were issued in ordinary shares. In addition, the Company issued money bonds aggregating £8,000.

The iron ore worked by the Whitehaven Mining Company, which included magnetite and "kidney" ore, occurred in pockets in the metamorphosed granite in the Great Fault which runs through the top of the Eskdale Valley. The two main workings were at Nab Ghyll, close to Boot Village and at Ghyll Foss on Birker Fell. The latter is on the south side of the valley, opposite Boot. One or two other trial drifts were also made, notably at Christcliff and Brantrake, the latter being on the south side of the valley, below Boot and away from the railway. Here good quality ore was proved, but working was not developed.

In 1876 it was decided to introduce a passenger service and this commenced operations in November, 1876. From this date the intermediate stations on the line (four in number) were as follows:— Muncaster Mill (1¼ miles); Irton Road (4 miles); Eskdale Green (4 miles); and Beckfoot (6 miles from Ravenglass). Muncaster Mill was more in the nature of a "halt," but there was a single siding, facing Ravenglass, at the other intermediate stations. At Boot there was a running-round loop and siding leading to the loading ramp at which ore from the Nab Ghyll Mine could be tipped into the wagons.

In order to tap the Ghyll Foss working, a branch line was laid from a point roughly midway between Beckfoot and Boot. This turned away to the south across the valley floor, passing in front of six brick cottages built specially by the Whitehaven Mining Company to house the men working the various drifts. Thereafter the track crossed the main road up the valley and and ran between substantial stone walls to the River Esk. Here an iron girder bridge carried it over the river to the Ghyll Foss drift. This bridge is still extant today and can be crossed with difficulty. The wooden baulks laid across the girder have largely rotted away, but the iron work is in fair order. The Ghyll Foss branch was abandoned in 1877 when the Whitehaven Mining Company failed.

Due to the latter happening, "Owd Ratty" was placed in the hands of a Receiver and Manager, who continued to operate the line. Nab Ghyll mine continued to be worked on a limited scale and a fair amount of seasonal passenger traffic was carried.

Throughout its length the Ravenglass & Eskdale Railway is quite severely, graded, especially from the point of view of the 15-inch gauge engines which were to take over after 1915. Starting from Ravenglass, which is 35 feet above sea-level, the line first follows the south side of the River Mite, drops to 17 feet, and rises again to 20 feet at Muncaster Mill. During this first fall, there is three chains of 1 in 50, followed by thirteen chains of 1 in 104. Incidentally, from Ravenglass to Eskdale Green the railway does not follow the Eskdale valley, but runs along the foot of Muncaster Fell (760 feet), which separates the rivers Mite and Esk.

Just beyond Muncaster Mill there is a practically continuous climb to Irton Road, which is 127 feet above sea-level. There are long stretches of 1 in 78 and 1 in 81, with shorter portions of 1 in 35, 1 in 40, 50 and 55.

From Irton Road the track falls for most of the three-quarters of a mile to Eskdale Green. From the latter there is a short sharp climb of 1 in 44 up Hollinghow Bank. Onwards to Beckfoot the gradients are of a switchback nature, but mainly against the locomotives, varying from 1 in 55 to 1 in 160, with one fairly long stretch of 1 in 75. Beckfoot station is 148 feet above sea level and 1¾ miles beyond Eskdale Green.

DEVON near Murthwaite with a down train for Ravenglass. Note the absence of a brake van.
Photograph: Mary C. Fair.

Beckfoot Station. The station buildings here, and at Boot, Eskdale Green and Muncaster were virtually identical but Beckfoot also had a goods shed and platform, seen on the left.
Postcard: Wrench Series.

In the last three-quarters of a mile "Owd Ratty" climbed another 62 feet to Boot Terminus, by gradients varying from 1 in 34 to 1 in 64 (minimum). Here the Whitehaven Mining Company built a row of cottages to house the miners and a little way beyond was the iron ore loading stage and run-round loop. Later on, after the Narrow Gauge Railways took over, most of the section between Beckfoot and Boot was to be abandoned and a short portion of the original track of the Ghyll Foss mineral branch utilised instead. The original Boot terminus was 210 feet above sea-level.

To work the ore traffic when the line was first opened, an 0-6-0 side tank engine was purchased from Manning Wardle & Company of Leeds. This locomotive, which had outside cylinders 10 x 16 ins., was Works No. 545 and was named "Devon." The following year, after a passenger service had been introduced, a second engine of similar dimensions and wheel notation was obtained from the same makers. This one was named "Nab Ghyll"[1] and was Works No. 629. These two tank engines comprised the locomotive power of "Owd Ratty" throughout its precarious existence. *Note: "owd" = old.*

Stations on the line, apart from Ravenglass and Irton Road, were of a primitive character. At Ravenglass, the platform had an "all over" wooden roof, and this survived a number of years after "Laal Ratty" came into existence. Short stone-flagged platforms were erected at all stations, but only at Irton Road was there a stone-built waiting-room and ticket office. At the other stations there was a small wooden hut, painted dull red, divided into a waiting-room and small ticket-cum-parcels office. The latter was presumably kept locked and tickets would be issued from it by the guard of the train which called there. *Note: '"Laal" = small.*

There were only six bridges over the line, and one main under-bridge (as there are today). The latter, a girder one, carries the track over the main road leading into Ravenglass village. The line passes under the main Whitehaven – Millom road at Muncaster Mill; under a bye-road at Irton Road and under the main road up the Eskdale Valley at Eskdale Green. All these

1. *Although the correct geographical name is "Nab Ghyll" the locomotive was actually named NABB GILL.*

are substantial stone-built affairs. The others, wooden structures with stone sides and falling into decay today, carry farm tracks between fields. They are located below Muncaster Mill, between Murthwaite and Irton Road, and between Eskdale Green and Beckfoot.

To work the passenger service provided "Owd Ratty" had four coaches, one of which was described as a "Pullman" and for first class fares. The line was operated on the "one engine in steam" principle.

The following service was provided during the winter of 1877-1878. First and third class accommodation was provided and on the first train up the dale parliamentary fares were charged. Mails were carried by this working, and most trains were "mixed." There were no Sunday trains.

	a.m.	p.m.		Th.o. a.m.	p.m.	p.m.
Ravenglass	dep. 8.35	4.30	Boot	dep.7.25	10.45	5.30
Muncaster Mill	8.40	4.35	Beckfoot	7.30	10.50	5.35
Irton Road	8.56	4.50	Eskdale Green	7.45	11.05	5.50
Eskdale Green	9.00	4.55	Irton Road	7.50	11.15	6.00
Beckfoot	9.15	5.10	Muncaster Mill	8.10	11.30	6.15
Boot	arr. 9.20	5.15	Ravenglass	arr. 8.15	11.40	6.20

It will be noted that travel by "Owd Ratty" was anything but speedy, and in addition to the booked stops, locomotives took water at the tank midway between Eskdale Green and Boot, where a convenient mountain stream was tapped.

The early morning turn from Boot on Thursdays only was put on for the benefit of dalesfolk wishing to go to Whitehaven Market, and this connected with a similar Furness train at Ravenglass.

During the summer months the time-table was expanded, and included a Sunday service. During the summer an "express" from Ravenglass to Boot, calling only at Irton Road, was put on. The full time-table for the summer of 1878 is reproduced as follows:–

Up			*Weekdays*				*Sundays*	
Ravenglass,	8.35	10.30	12.30	4.30	8.05	10.00	4.00	6.15
Muncaster	8.40	–	12.35	4.35	8.10	10.05	4.05	6.20
Irton Road	8.50	10.50	12.55	4.50	8.25	10.20	4.20	6.35
Eskdale Green	9.00	–	1.05	4.55	8.30	10.25	4.25	6.40
Beckfoot	9.15	–	1.25	5.10	8.45	10.40	4.40	6.55
Boot	9.20	11.10	1.30	5.15	8.50	10.45	4.45	7.00

Down								
Boot	9.30	11.20	2.10	5.30	8.55	12.05	5.00	7.15
Beckfoot	9 35	11.25	2.15	5.35	9.00	12.10	5.05	7.25
Eskdale Green	9.50	11.40	2.35	5.50	9.15	12.25	5.20	7.30
Irton Road	10.00	11.45	2.45	6.00	9.20	12.35	5.30	7.40
Muncaster	10.15	12.00	3.05	6.15	9.35	12.50	5.45	7.55
Ravenglass	10.20	12.05	3.10	6.20	9.40	12.55	5.50	8.00

On the first trip up and down the dale, parliamentary and first class fares were charged; on the rest first and third class.

The above time-table, with only slight variations, represented "Owd Ratty's" summer service until the closure of the line. Below is given the standard Winter time-table as operating, on weekdays only, during the winter of 1880-81 and thereafter:—

Ravenglass	6.30	8.35	12.15	4.32	Boot	7.25	9.30	2.10	5.30
Muncaster	6.35	8.40	12.20	4.35	Beckfoot	7.30	9.35	2.15	5.35
Irton Road	6.50	8.56	12.35	4.50	Eskdale Green	7.45	9.50	2.35	5.50
Eskdale Green	6.55	9.00	12.45	4.55	Irton Road	7.50	9.55	2.45	6.00
Beckfoot	7.10	9.15	1.00	5.10	Muncaster	8.10	10.10	3.05	6.15
Boot	7.15	9.20	1.05	5.15	Ravenglass	8.15	10.15	3.10	6.20

The first trip up and down the dale ran on Thursdays only.

The Ravenglass & Eskdale Railway Company, as such, was formed after the failure of the Whitehaven Mining Company by Mr. Robert Woodley of Whitehaven, together with three other local gentlemen. A brother of the chairman, Mr. Sydney Woodley, was appointed manager and held that post until 1896 when he went as Traffic Manager to the Lancashire, Derbyshire & East Coast Railway (later the Great Central Railway). Yet another brother, Mr. Lewis W. Woodley, acted as manager from 1896 until 1911, the line having been run in Chancery for some time during that period.

The big house at Miteside, between Muncaster Mill and Murthwaite, had its own station with a 'waiting room' adapted from an old sailing boat.
Postcard: Wrench Series.

In both 3 ft. and 15 in. gauge days Irton Road was the principle source of local goods traffic
with a small yard opposite the platform.
Postcard: Wrench Series No. 5513.

The trouble that dogged the steps of "Owd Ratty" was the lack of money to convert the line to a mainly passenger carrying concern. The original promoters were purely concerned with mineral carrying and facilities for passenger traffic were only an afterthought. Thus, when the iron mines closed, the R. & E.R. had to rely on seasonal tourist traffic for the bulk of its revenue. This traffic grew steadily in volume, but "Owd Ratty" lacked rolling stock to cope with it. The following revenue figures for the decade 1898-1907 tell their own story:—

Year	Passenger Revenue	Goods Revenue	Total
1898	£742	£318	£1060
1899	732	412	1144
1900	761	282	1043
1901	804	310	1114
1902	765	376	1141
1903	865	365	1220
1904	860	354	1214
1905	816	377	1191
1906	787	368	1155
1907	786	337	1133

On these revenue figures "Owd Ratty" was barely keeping its head above water.

In 1908 there was a prospect of the iron mines at Boot being re-opened. Furthermore, the inhabitants of the upper Eskdale valley were anxious that their main contact with the outside world should be at least maintained, if not strengthened and improved. The prime mover in a reconstruction scheme which was put forward for the approval of the Court of Chancery was Mr. John Musgrave, of Wastdale Hall.

A Prospectus issued in July, 1908 stated it was anticipated that the iron mines would resume production and the development of stone quarry traffic (from Beckfoot) was also probable. It was also considered that the time had arrived when provision should be made for the equipment of the line by reinstatement of the permanent way and the purchase of "light railway cars" and additional locomotives, whereby the demands of the summer traffic might be suitably met. Mention was made of the fact that in the height of the summer season, even some of the mineral wagons had to be pressed into passenger service but even these were often insufficient to cope with the volume of traffic. This circumstance had not encouraged the management to advertise the beauty of Eskdale or to encourage tourists to use the line.

An estimate was prepared by the management for relaying about four miles of track with new steel rails of 45 lbs. per yard and re-sleepering with creosoted sleepers; for providing three new passenger coaches and an additional engine at a cost of about £6,000; together with certain monies required to repay advances and costs of the Chancery proceedings and put an end thereto, thus enabling the Company, with a new Board of Directors, to resume control.

It was proposed to issue first mortgage debenture stock to the extent of £8,000, being a first charge on the railway and its equipment, and bearing interest at 7% per annum.

According to the Master's certificate, the claims under money bonds and other creditors amounted to £16,640, and it was proposed to issue preferred ordinary shares of £1 each, paying 5% in settlement of these claims in the following proportions:–

1. For every £8 of debenture stock subscribed by the creditor, issue first preference shares in proportion of £1 share for each £4 of claim.

2. To issue to those not subscribing for debenture stock preferred ordinary shares of £1 each at 5% to the extent of 2/6d in the £ upon the admitted claim.

3. To the ordinary shareholders one deferred ordinary share of £1 for every twenty old shares at the rate of 1/- in the £ to be allotted to the holders of existing ordinary shares.

The issue of the £8,000 7% debentures was commended for subscription in the following terms:–

"To those who are interested in the preservation of the railway and the development of the district of the Eskdale Valley, Cumberland, stated to be one of the most beautiful in England.

"To those who have made advances on money bonds, and who are creditors, with the object of giving a value to their claims as well as to the shareholders who in a deferred degree are interested in the property.

"To the investing public the issue, although speculative, has a strong probability of success, coupled with the fact that it is a first charge on a railway which has been established by Act of Parliament. The foregoing data show that with a comparatively small increase of revenue the payment of interest is assured."

Eskdale Express derailed at Murthwaite

The line inevitably had its share of minor accidents. Fortunately no one was hurt on this occasion when DEVON was derailed beside the now demolished Murthwaite Farm on March 10th, 1905. Postcard: R. & E.R. Historical Series No. 5.

The latter statement is borne out by the fact that in 1903 the receipts (£1,220) just balanced the expenditure, although in 1907 they fell short by £120. Finally, it was proposed on the completion of the works in question that a sinking fund for the payment off of the debentures of £200 per annum would be instituted which should pay off the debenture stock in 25 years at a rate of 4%. Until payment off or redemption of the debentures the holders were to have the right of appointing two-thirds of the directors, together with voting powers in the Company at the rate of one vote for each £1 invested.

At the same time as this general appeal was made to the public, the Receiver and Manager of "Owd Ratty" approached the Furness Railway regarding the relaying of the track and provision of new rolling stock. The precedent for this action was the fact that the Furness Company, in their Parliamentary Bill for 1899 had originally included clauses empowering them to work, lease or purchase the R.& E.R. The latter were afterwards ordered by the Directors to be struck out of the Bill as the result of a petition by Mr. Woodley. He objected because the Furness Company had not scheduled an agreement to the Bill providing for the terms of such working, lease or purchase.

Probably with the thought in their minds that previous overtures had been rejected, the Furness Board, when they received the R.& E.R. request in 1908, decided to take no action. They replied that they had no statutory powers to subscribe to, or to work or purchase the light

A late view of the original 0-6-0T DEVON (Manning Wardle 545 of 1875).
Note the Westinghouse air brake which was fitted by Furness Railway Co. staff from Moor Row shed.
Photograph: Collection A. Neale.

railway undertaking. Furthermore, the Company considered that in any event they would retain a considerable proportion of the passengers using the Ravenglass and Eskdale line.

The refusal of the Furness Company to take over "Owd Ratty" was the final "death blow" to the little railway, since the response of the general public to the prospectus previously outlined was meagre. The iron mines at Boot worked fitfully for a couple of years, but the line remained closed to passenger traffic. In 1912 the mines ceased operations and "Owd Ratty" closed down entirely, after a chequered career of just under 40 years. Three years were to elapse before its diminutive successor took over.

Opposite page: In the last days of the three foot gauge railway maintenance was minimal
as can be seen from this view of Muncaster Station.
Photograph: Collection A. Neale.

CHAPTER TWO
"LAAL RATTY," 1915-1925

SANS PAREIL poses at Ravenglass about 1915 with the entire stock available at that time – seven Bassett-Lowke coaches (ex Oslo), Heywood coach and brakevan plus three Heywood open wagons.
Note the abandoned 3 ft. gauge siding in the foreground.
Collection: A. Neale.

IN the previous chapter we have seen how "Owd Ratty" struggled fitfully on from 1908 to 1912 and finally gave up the struggle for existence. The line then lay derelict for three years.

In 1915, Narrow Gauge Railways Limited, which company had been started by the late Robert P. Mitchell, became aware of the abandoned railway in the Eskdale valley. Mr. Mitchell, together with Mr. W. J. Bassett-Lowke, had gained considerable experience in working 15in. gauge miniature railways at Rhyl, Geneva, Oslo and Fairbourne. A visit was paid to Ravenglass by Mr. Mitchell in June, 1915, and the line inspected. He found desolation rampant. All the 3 ft. track was *in situ*, but very heavily overgrown. At some points notably Muncaster Mill, grass completely obscured the rails. Many of the sleepers had rotted away and the station buildings were in a dilapidated condition. Some of the coaches still stood under the covered roof of Ravenglass station.

In spite of this gloomy prospect, coupled with the fact that the 1914-18 war was in full swing, it was decided to take over the line and get at least a portion of it working by August of the same year. In order to facilitate this, rails and sleepers, where they were good enough, were used for the narrower gauge. Many of the latter, although rotted away where the rails had been spiked down to the wider gauge, were sound nearer the centre and quite satisfactory for further use.

Clearance and conversion work started at the end of June and seven weeks later the scale model locomotive "Sans Pareil" commenced working passenger traffic as far as Muncaster Mill and back. Progress beyond this point was naturally slow on account of the war-time difficulties in obtaining materials, and other restrictions. Nevertheless Irton Road was reach in 1916 and Boot the following year.

Passenger traffic during the holiday season grew steadily in volume and the diminutive size of the railway proved an added attraction to visitors and a big "selling point" for "Laal Ratty," as the line was now named by the dalesfolk.

The locomotive stud was increased during the first three years by four additional engines; the scale model 4-6-2 "Colossus" and three Heywood side tanks (coal burning), "Katie," "Ella" and "Muriel." In 1919 another scale model, "Sir Aubrey Brocklebank" (4-6-2) was added. These, and subsequent locomotives, are fully described in Chapter V.

Goods traffic also grew steadily in volume and to quite respectable proportions. At first it was customary to attach the odd wagon of coal, timber or merchandise to a passenger train, thus converting it into a "mixed." Later, however, regular goods trips were run.

A posed view of SANS PAREIL and a short train at Muncaster soon after the reopening.
The makeshift nature of the regauging of the track from 3 ft. gauge is most evident in this picture.
The original 40 lb. per yard rail has simply been moved on the original and none too sound sleepers.
Photograph: Whitehaven News, 16th September 1915.

A Bank Holiday in 1923 and everything possible is being used to carry the crowds of passengers. ELLA and a well filled train of Theakston stone wagons are seen about to leave the original passenger station at Ravenglass. Postcard: R. & E.R. Historical Series No. 2.

Until 1922 the goods traffic handled by "Laal Ratty" consisted mainly of coal, coke, cattle food and general merchandise up the Eskdale Valley and pit props and sawn timber from Irton Road down to Ravenglass. In 1922 there was a new development. Just short of Beckfoot station a red granite quarry was opened out and this has been worked on an increasing scale down to the present day. Not only has this quarry provided steady employment for a number of men, but it has ensured a steady all-the-year-round source of traffic to the R. & E.R. This is especially valuable to a concern whose passenger traffic is very largely of a seasonal character.

With the opening of the quarry at Beckfoot, a crushing and treating plant for the stone had to be erected. Bearing in mind the importance of preserving the beauty of the Eskdale Valley and avoiding the erection of unsightly buildings, the Company sought as unobtrusive a site for the crushing plant as possible. Eventually a spot about midway between Irton Road and Muncaster Mill stations was decided upon. Taking its name from a nearby farm, Murthwaite Crushing Plant is tucked in at the foot of Muncaster Fell. There is no road near and having a northern aspect little sunshine falls directly on it, which tends to make the plant even Less noticeable. Murthwaite stands at the foot of a "dip." This enabled a loop line to be constructed at the eastern end of the dip. The line leading to the crusher runs along a stone embankment, 600 ft. long and terminates on a 100 ft. row of concrete pillars which are 15 ft. above the level of the main line. At the end of this high-level track the stone is tipped into the crusher where it is ingeniously sorted and graded into seven different sizes before reloading into wagons at the opposite end and below the plant. The graded stone was conveyed in narrow gauge wagons

An official R. & E.R. postcard of a train running through Mitredale, looking across to the slopes of Scafell.

(including some special bogie units, described in Chapter five) until 1929. The present-day arrangements, which date from that year, are described in Chapter three.

Having described the goods and mineral traffic handled by "Laal Ratty," let us take a look at the passenger traffic developments from 1915 to 1925.

When the line was first opened in the summer of 1915, trains ran more or less "as required." The novelty of such a minute railway, coupled with the delightful scenery through which the line runs, gave "Laal Ratty " a double appeal. Once the opening right through to Boot was completed, a regular timetable came into force and from 1920 onwards it has had a permanent place in "Bradshaw." At Bank holiday periods the resources of the Company were often sorely taxed and the mid-morning train up the dale, which left Ravenglass after the arrival of main line trains from Whitehaven and Barrow, frequently ran in two, or even three, portions. Under such circumstances the second or third portion sometimes had to be entrusted to such an uncertain quantity as "Katie." A good story is told of the vagaries of this Heywood 0-4-0, whose lack of steaming qualities were notorious. The occasion was the Fell Dales Show, held annually at Boot, and the year was either 1918 or 1919. At all events the crowds were unprecedented and every locomotive and carriage which "Laal Ratty" could muster had to be pressed into service. At the close of the Show, "Katie" set out for Ravenglass with a packed train. Hardly was she through Beckfoot than she ran short of steam. Among the passengers was a quartette of bookmakers who had been attending the Show Hound Trail. Among their "luggage" was a small table. The evening was fine and they evidently grew weary of sitting in the train while Katie's driver endeavoured to raise steam. They therefore got out of the coach, set up their table and canvas stools and commenced a game of cards! "Katie's" behaviour must, however, be regarded as an exception, since she was the only locomotive which gave consistent trouble in service. The other Heywood engines, "Ella" and "Muriel" were not up to the standard of scale models in performance, but they did well on goods running and relief passenger work.

From the time the R.& E.R. was re-opened up to Boot, the Mails for Eskdale were carried. "Owd Ratty" handled them until she faded out and from then until 1917 they were conveyed by horse and cart from Drigg station on the Fumess Railway. The Mail contract expired in 1928, when the Post Office started running their own Motor Mail Van from Holmrook P.O.

Several innovations took place in 1922. Until that year there were no turning facilities at either Ravenglass or Boot. This involved tender-first running in one direction, which could be extremely unpleasant during the wetter weather which inflicts the Eskdale Valley at often too frequent intervals, and during the winter months. A turntable was therefore put in at Ravenglass and one at Boot. At the same time as the latter was put in, the final portion of the line from Beckfoot to Boot, which involved the steep climb up behind and past the miners' cottages, was abandoned. Instead the track terminated in front of the cottages, along the initial course of the old Foss Ghyll branch. The turntable was put in here and one of the cottages was turned into a tea-room.

The Company embarked on another venture in 1922 which was to prove very successful. This was a motor-coach trip from Irton Road station to Wastwater and back. The coach left

The new 15 in. gauge line originally terminated near Dalegarth cottages before being extended to the present
terminus in 1926. In this early view, COLOSSUS and train wait to return to Ravenglass.
Note the ex-Duffield Bank track sections dumped on the right.
Postcard: Abraham's Series – 789.

Above: For a period between the two World Wars the railway provided a useful freight service for the valley. This included considerable timber traffic. In this early 1920's view piles of sawn logs are being loaded up in the sidings at Irton Road.
Photograph: Collection A. Neale.

Below: In the early 1920's the Heywood 0-6-0T ELLA saw constant use until finally withdrawn, completely worn out, in 1927. Here shown backing a train of stone up to Murthwaite, 11th August 1924.
Photograph: H. G. W. Household.

The unique 4-6-0+0-6-4 RIVER MITE leaves Eskdale Green with a well loaded train. It was built at Murthwaite in 1927 using parts from SANS PAREIL, COLOSSUS and SIR AUBREY BROCKLEBANK with a new boiler from the Yorkshire Engine Company. Problems with the frames caused the loco to be withdrawn at the end of the 1937 season and dismantled for a complete rebuild. This was never carried out due to the onset of World War 2, the two chassis being sold and the boiler dumped.
Postcard: R.& E.R Historical Series No. 4.

Irton Road after the arrival of the mid-morning train from Ravenglass and returned there to connect with the late afternoon trip down the dale. The route followed from Irton Road was via Irton Pike, Santon Bridge and Netherwastdale.

Slip coach working on the morning "express" from Ravenglass was instituted in the summer of 1923, when a couple of coaches carrying Irton Road passengers only were attached to the rear of the train and "slipped" in the approved style. Introduced more or less as a novelty, slip coach working was abandoned in 1925 .

During the winter months the passenger train service was reduced to the morning and evening "mail" trips, plus a "market special" on Thursdays only. The latter only was steam-hauled as a rule, the petrol "scooter" doing the mail runs. Goods traffic, run when required, was also steam-hauled: usually by one of the Heywood tanks, or by the 4-4-2 scale model "Sans Pareil." On one occasion, Driver John Lister, who had been employed in a similar capacity with "Owd Ratty," did a notable piece of work with "Sans Pareil." Old John was really the foreman fitter with the narrow gauge line and only drove on occasions. On the trip in question, he had worked a "special," consisting of the four-wheeled ex-Dynometer car and an open coach, up to Dalegarth. He was just setting off again for Ravenglass and carrying three passengers when one of "San Pareil's" connecting rods broke. Nothing daunted, Lister tied up the valve in the central position, by means of a piece of wire lashed to the chimney, and worked his engine back to Ravenglass on one cylinder! To ease the weight, the covered coach was dropped off at Eskdale Green siding (the first one to make a trailing connection towards Ravenglass), but "Sans Pareil" reached Ravenglass on time.

During the period 1917-1925, steady progress was made with the relaying and renovating of the track. As previously stated, a number of the sleepers used by the 3 ft. gauge line were utilised for the 1 ft. 3 in. track, since they were quite sound towards their centre although largely rotted away where the original rails had rested on them. Gradually they in turn were replaced by new ones and, after the Beckfoot quarry commenced operations, a start was made to ballast the track more thoroughly. This led to smoother and more comfortable running.

Another job to be tackled was the re-fencing of the line almost throughout its entire length. Both the wooden posts and wire of the original fencing had either rotted away or collapsed in many places, with the result that stray sheep, and sometimes cattle, wandered on to the track and held up traffic until they were chased back into the fields or on to the fell sides.

Signalling as such does not exist on "Laal Ratty," but in the early days, mainly to add a touch of realism, a pair of scale model starting signals were erected at Ravenglass. They acted in conjunction with the points, which were hand-worked, and were of the two-post bracket type. A similar pair acted as splitting stop signals at Irton Road. Both examples were removed in the late 1920's.

With the opening up of the Murthwaite Crusher Plant in 1923, some modification of the track layout at Ravenglass was required. A high-level siding was put in, with a loop at the end,

COLOSSUS has a somewhat mixed train of stock in this commercial postcard view including a Heywood open wagon for sundry freight and a mixture of Bassett-Lowke and Heywood open passenger stock. Postcard: Collection A. Neale.

leading on to a "tippler gear" which emptied the special hopper wagons supplied by Theakston's, of London, into the main line wagons, which were run in under the tipping apparatus.

Right from the outset the original 3 ft. gauge engine shed was used for the same purpose by smaller locomotives and a workshop was also established there. Later this was moved to Murthwaite. A substantial wooden carriage shed was also erected at Ravenglass.

Some details of the management and staff of "Laal Ratty" in its early days may be of interest. As already stated the first General Manager was Mr. R. Proctor Mitchell, a keen model railway engineer. The Secretary was Mr. H. Wills, who later went to manage the Fairbourne Miniature Railway near Barmouth, in Wales. The first Superintendent of the Line was Mr. "Bob" Hardie. He was a notable character and had travelled widely. Among his lesser known exploits was the winning of a prize at the Chicago World Fair, in the early days of the present century, for shaving a man most perfectly in the shortest possible time. He was a genial soul and later went to take up a similar post with the Romney, Hythe & Dymchurch Railway in Kent.

Over the "motive power department" presided Mr. W. V. Cauchi as engineer. Messrs. Johnson and John Lister were the fitters. The latter had been a driver with "Owd Ratty" and did a certain amount on the miniature line. He usually handled "Muriel." John Lowther was "Ella's" regular driver. His father had been with the original line and continued with the new, as Goods Manager. Fred Thompson and Bert Seed were respectively the regular drivers of "Sir Aubrey Brocklebank" and "Colossus." There were also one or two spare drivers for the "summer rush," including Peter LeNeve Poster, a young apprentice engineer, who usually handled the 4-4-2 "Sans Pareil." A few years before his retirement, John Lister gave up driving entirely and took over the running of the oil engine which drives the Murthwaite Crusher. His chief handicap was deafness, brought on in the early days of the 1914-18 war when he drove a locomotive at the gun testing plant of Messrs. Vickers-Armstrong at Eskmeals, near Ravenglass.

Until 1927 the R. & E.R. locomotives had a variety of liveries. All the Heywood tanks were painted green and had polished brass domes. Nameplates were brass with raised brass lettering. "Sans Pareil" was originally painted red, and since she often ran in "double harness" with "Sir Aubrey Brocklebank," the latter was painted the same colour. "Colossus," on the other hand, ran in blue livery. From the time "River Esk" went into traffic, the colour scheme was changed to Great Western Green, at the instigation of the then chairman of the Company, Sir Aubrey Brocklebank, who was also associated with the G.W.R.

The Bassett-Lowke and Heywood coaches were originally finished in a teak colour, but later this was altered to the present shade of Midland red.

CHAPTER THREE
"LAAL RATTY," 1925-1939

RIVER ESK pauses at Eskdale Green with a short train. For some years between the wars the railway provided a vital freight service to local farmers, hence the train of Heywood opens in the adjoining siding. Photograph: Collection A. Neale.

BY the year 1925 "Laal Ratty" can be said to have settled down to steady operations. The early "improvisation" period was now over. Most of the track had been relaid and re-sleepered; and during the next two years certain engines were to be scrapped and others rebuilt, as related in the next chapter.

Meanwhile a further improvement was carried out at the Boot end of the line. It has already been stated that the last portion of the track from Beckfoot to Boot was abandoned in 1922 on account of the steep gradient and the line terminated in front of the old miners' cottages at Dalegarth, just at the commencement of the original Ghyll Foss mineral branch. In 1926 it was decided to extend the metals still further along the original Ghyll Foss track to the point where the latter crossed the main road up the dale. At one time it had been hoped to take "Laal Ratty" across the road and further up the valley, but certain legal difficulties about the road crossing loomed up and this project had to be abandoned. The new extension therefore terminated by the boundary of the main road and here a new luncheon and tea-room was erected to replace that which had been made in one of the empty miner's cottages. There is a single platform and running-round loop, ending on the turntable which was moved to this site in 1927.

In 1926 the first through bookings from stations on the London Midland & Scottish Railway commenced. At first their range was limited to stations as far as Whitehaven (both direct and via the old "Joint Line" through Egremont and Moor Row) to the north and to Barrow southward. Later, all stations between Carnforth and Workington were included. Finally, on account of the popularity of the Eskdale Valley for day excursionists from Lancashire, through bookings were instituted from Morecambe.

Close to Beckfoot station is the Stanley Ghyll Hotel of the Co-operative Holiday Association, which opens every year from Whitsuntide to the end of September. It is invariably full throughout the season and since the guests generally arrive and depart in large parties, "specials" are frequently run to and from Beckfoot by the R.& E.R.

It has already been noted that the Mail contract terminated in 1928, when the Post Office commenced running their own motor-van up the Dale. Furthermore, motor-coaches were now invading even the fastness of Eskdale, and while there is not even today a daily bus service a special coach commenced running to Whitehaven on Thursdays (Market Day) and Saturdays. This meant that passenger traffic during the winter months fell to the slenderest proportions. In view of this, winter services were withdrawn after 1928. A limited service was run at Easter and the full summer service came into operation at Whitsuntide and continued until the end of September. Today, the Easter running is discontinued, and passenger traffic commences at Whitsuntide. The table in operation just before the outbreak of the World War is given below.

		WEEKDAYS							SUNDAYS	
Up		Th.o.	S.o.	X	X	Y	S.o.	K	Z	Z
Ravenglass	dep.	7.40	9.30	10.55	12.30	3.05	4.20	6.55	11.45	2.25
Irton Road	...	8.00	9.50	11.15	12.50	3.25	4.40	7.15	12.05	2.45
Eskdale Green	...	8.03	9.55	11.20	12.55	3.30	4.45	7.20	12.10	2.50
Beckfoot	...	8.10	10.10	11.35	1.10	3.45	4.55	7.30	12.25	3.05
Dalegarth	arr.	8.15	10.15	11.40	1.15	3.50	5.00	7.35	12.30	3.10
Down		Th.o.	S.o.	X	M		N	Z	Z	Z
Dalegarth	dep.	8.20	10.20	11.45	2.00	5.05	7.45	12.35	5.00	6.45
Beckfoot	...	8.22	10.25	11.47	2.02	5.07	7.47	12.37	5.02	6.47
Eskdale Green	...	8.30	10.35	11.55	2.10	5.15	7.55	12.45	5.10	6.55
Irton Road	...	8.35	10.40	12.00	2.15	5.20	8.00	12.50	5.15	7.00
Ravenglass	arr.	8.55	11.00	12.30	2.40	5.45	8.20	1.10	5.40	7.20

NOTES.—Th.o. Thursdays only.   S.o. Saturdays only.

X Runs 10 minutes later on Saturday and 40 minutes later on Thursdays until September 7th.

Y Does not run on September 9th and 16th.

K Daily to September 2nd; Saturdays only after.

M Runs 40 minutes earlier on Wednesdays, 5th and 19th July; August 2nd, 16th and 30th; and September 13th.

Z Not after September 10th.

N Except Saturdays and not after September 1st.

Up trains called at Beckfoot to set down only and down trains to pick up only.

The Sunday service ceased on September 10th. The somewhat extensive variations in the time-table on certain specific dates were arranged to suit the arrival and departure of large parties of

Above: There were tremendous traffic peaks at times such as Bank Holidays when double heading became necessary in the early days. SANS PAREIL and COLOSSUS pull away from Eskdale Green with one such heavily loaded train. Postcard: W. J. Bassett-Lowke No. 1355.

Below: The railway had an important visitor in June 1925 when Captain J. E. P. Howey's new Pacific locomotive GREEN GODDESS arrived for trial running prior to the opening of the Romney, Hythe & Dymchurch Railway. The locomotive's designer, Henry Greenly, poses on the footplate outside Ravenglass Engine shed. Postcard: R. & E.R. Historical Series No. 3.

The line's great locomotive rebuilding success was RIVER IRT. Transformed from the Heywood 0-8-0T
MURIEL in 1927 she is seen soon after completion about to depart from Dalegarth.
Her nameplates were not fitted until the following year. Postcard: Collection A. Neale.

Below: In the early days crushed stone from the plant at Murthwaite was transferred to standard gauge
wagons via a neat rotary tipper supplied by Francis Theakston Limited of Crewe. It can clearly be seen
behind RIVER IRT and her train but was replaced about this time (1927) when new bogie hopper wagons
came into use. Later still the standard gauge line was extended up to Murthwaite itself.
Postcard: Sankey D885/201.

RIVER IRT hauls a packed train over the 'mixed gauge' section between Ravenglass and Murthwaite sometime in the 1930's. The standard gauge track was installed in 1929 and removed after stone traffic ceased in 1953. Postcard: Sankey E830/201.

guests at the Stanley Ghyll Hotel, Beckfoot. As in the days of "Owd Ratty," the Whitehaven market train on Thursdays only was still put on.

It will be noted that Muncaster Mill station no longer appears in the timetable. Since it only served its name-sake and another cottage close by, plus the fact that both buildings are adjacent to the main road along which a bus service operates, Muncaster Mill was closed some years before the war.

An interesting event took place in 1925. The scale model Pacific "Green Goddess," designed by Captain Howey, carried out her trials on the R.& E.R. prior to going to the R.H. & D.R.

In the meantime one of the most trying gradients for the heavily loaded passenger trains from Ravenglass was that commencing at Muncaster Mill. The steepest portion, before the gradient eases out at Miteside, runs through a plantation and in bad weather this fact aggravated the "wet rail" bogey. It was therefore decided to "shave" the top off this bank, thus easing the climb at the most troublesome point. This work was successfully carried out, the track level being lowered by several feet and a neat new concrete bridge made over a small tributary of the River Mite which passed below the railway. This work was completed during 1925-26.

Further improvements were also carried out at Ravenglass. The wooden roof over the station, which had survived from the days of "Owd Ratty," was removed and a new booking office erected on the footpath approach from Ravenglass (L.M.S.) station, through the goods yard of the latter.

Amongst the R. & E.R.'s more surprising claims to fame was that it was the first public railway in Britain to employ a standard gauge diesel shunting locomotive, necessitated by the decision in 1929 to extend standard gauge rails to Murthwaite. Built by Kerr Stuart (KS 4429) in 1929 this 6wDM was highly successful. Photographed on 8th May 1954, by which time it stone traffic had ceased, it was sold the following year and put in many more years industrial service with various owners before ultimate preservation.
Photograph: F. W. Shuttleworth.

In the year 1929 came the final stage in the pre-war development of "Laal Ratty." This was the decision to carry a normal 4 ft. 8½ in. track from Ravenglass up to Murthwaite Crusher (2 miles). The reason for this was fairly obvious, since it meant cutting out one complete operation in the transportation of granite from Beckfoot Quarry to the main line wagons. Up to 1929 the untreated stone had been railed to Murthwaite, unloaded at the plant, reloaded after treatment, only to be transferred once again at Ravenglass. The latter operation had been speeded up from 1927 by the use of special 6-ton bogie hopper wagons, described in Chapter Five, but the method was rather cumbersome.

The next problem was how to lay the broad gauge track within the limits of the existing width of road bed available without involving any heavy earth work. The solution was to lay the 4 ft. 8½ in. track "astride" the 15 in. line giving it the appearance of a double line of narrow track.

From now on, all main line wagons were worked right up to Murthwaite and the special narrow gauge 6-ton bogie wagons were disposed of as indicated in the previous chapter. The rest of the 15 in. quarry wagons were all retained for traffic between Beckfoot Quarry and Murthwaite.

To handle the "broad gauge" traffic between Ravenglass and Murthwaite the R.& E.R. obtained an 0-6-0 Diesel locomotive from Kerr Stuart & Co. of Leeds. This unit is powered by a 90 h.p. airless injection McLaren Benz engine. Her six cylinders measure 135 mm. x 200 mm. and the normal engine speed is 800 r.p.m. The pistons are of cast iron and have four rings and a scraper. The cranks are set at 180 degrees and the governor speeds are 520-800 r.p.m. The chains are of the roller type and have a 2½ in. pitch. The locomotive has a fuel tank with a capacity of 42 gallons and weighs 15 tons in working order. She is painted green and lined out in yellow.

Many thousands of tons of granite are dealt with annually at the Murthwaite Crusher, from which "Big Ratty" hauls it in main line wagons to Ravenglass from whence it goes to many parts of Cumberland, Lancashire and Yorkshire. During the past 20 years "Beckfoot Granite" has earned itself an excellent reputation.

Shortly before the war broke out the Engineering, Carriage and Wagon shops were transferred from Ravenglass to Murthwaite and here all but the heaviest repairs are carried out. The locomotive shed remains at Ravenglass and here the narrow gauge steam engines and the passenger and one goods petrol unit are housed. Two more of the narrow gauge petrol locomotives and the broad gauge diesel unit are shedded at Murthwaite, and one of the former at Irton Road.

An overall view of the Murthwaite crushing plant and its associated standard and fifteen inch gauge sidings on 25th of May 1951. The Kerr Stuart diesel has been stripped right down for major overhaul necessitating narrow gauge haulage of the stone traffic in the interim.
Photograph: Brian Hilton.

CHAPTER FOUR

THE STEAM LOCOMOTIVES

Class 30 Bassett-Lowke 'Little Giant' 4-4-2 SANS PAREIL outside Ravenglass shed circa 1925. Note the dumped Douglas scooter in the background and the Heywood cast iron sleepered track in use for the sidings. Photograph: Collection W. H. Whitworth.

AS already stated, when Narrow Gauge Railway Limited commenced to work the Ravenglass & Eskdale Railway in 1915, traffic to and from Muncaster Mill was worked by the 4-4-2 scale model locomotive "Sans Pareil." This engine was built by Bassett-Lowke Limited, the well-known Northampton firm of model engineers, in 1912 to the designs of the late Mr. Henry Greenley. "Sans Pareil" was originally built for the Geneva Miniature Railway and was named "Prince Olaf" The following were her principal dimensions:—

Cylinders, $4\frac{1}{8}$ x $6\frac{1}{4}$ ins.; coupled wheels, 20 in. dia.; bogie wheels, $9\frac{3}{4}$ ins. dia.; trailing wheels, 10 $\frac{1}{4}$ ins. dia. Coupled axles had a diameter of $^{22}/_{16}$ ins. and the boiler barrel was $19\frac{3}{4}$ ins. dia. The length between tube plates was 4 ft. $3\frac{1}{2}$ ins. "Sans Pareil" had a wheelbase of 7 ft. 0 $\frac{3}{4}$ ins. and a tractive effort of 680 lbs. Here total heating surface was 11,000 square inches and working pressure 120 lbs.

To assist "Sans Pareil" in handling the rapidly increasing volume of traffic, a similar locomotive, but of the "Pacific" (4-6-2) type, was put in traffic towards the end of 1915. This was "Colossus," another Bassett-Lowke product and also designed by Greenley. Built in 1914 for Capt. Howey's private railway and named "John Anthony," this engine was renamed before coming to the Eskdale line. "Colossus" had a wheelbase of 8 ft. 5 ins. and the length of her boiler between the tube plates was 5 ft. 11½ ins.: otherwise she was dimensionally similar to "Sans Pareil." Her weight was 2 tons 18 cwt. Both these scale models had eight-wheeled bogie tenders carrying 50 gallons of water, and were coke fired.

"Colossus" soon proved her worth when she completed a test run, which comprised a complete double journey (up and down the Eskdale valley) of 13 miles in 90 minutes, including stops, on a consumption of 93 lbs. of coke and 50 gallons of water. The load hauled was an average one of 8½ tons. In "full size" figures this performance represents the lifting of a 500 ton train over a 52¼ mile run at an average speed of 35 m.p.h. (including stops). Considering the gradients of 1 in 50, 1 in 40 and 1 in 34 which "Colossus" had to negotiate, the performance can be regarded as a good one.

In the meantime, as the N.G.R. extended up the Eskdale valley, a fair amount of goods traffic developed. To handle this the Company obtained an 0-4-0 tank engine named "Katie," built originally for the Duke of Westminster's private railway at Eaton Hall, near Chester, in 1896. She was designed by the late Sir A. P. Heywood, of Duffield Bank, Derby, and was Duffield Works No. 4. "Katie" had two outside cylinders 4⅝ ins. x 7 ins., 15 in. dia. driving wheels and 70 sq. ft. of heating surface. Working pressure was 170 lbs. and weight 3 tons 5 cwt. "Katie" was a notoriously bad steamer and was soon sold to the Fairbourne Miniature Railway at Barmouth in Central Wales[1]. To replace "Katie," came two more Duffield Bank

1. *Not so – "Katie" was sold in 1919 to Llewelyn's Miniature Railway at Southport. The locomotive did not stay there long, being sold to the Fairbourne line in 1923.*

The final development of the Bassett-Lowke "Little Giant" was the 'Class 60' Pacific of which COLOSSUS was the sole example. After purchase from Captain Howey in 1916 she became the mainstay of the locomotive fleet for the next ten years. This view shows her after the front running plate had been modified in 1922 to carry extra sanding gear to cope with the heavy stone traffic.
Postcard: Bassett-Lowke.

Above: ELLA and MURIEL outside the shed at Ravenglass in 1925. The cab of the Theakston 'Crewe Tractor' can be seen in the background.

Below: Original 15 in. motive power in the form of 'scale' Bassett-Lowke SANS PAREIL contrasts sharply with the Heywood sisters, MURIEL and ELLA. Both photographs: W. H. Whitworth.

products, "Ella" (built 188, Works No. 2) and "Muriel" (built 1894, Works No. 3). "Ella" was an 0-6-0 tank with cylinders 6¼ x 8 ins., wheels 13½ ins. dia. and a wheelbase of 4 ft. 6 ins. She weighed 3 tons 15 cwt. "Muriel" was an 0-8-0 and had cylinders of the same size as "Ella," but her coupled wheels were 17½ ins. dia. and she weighed 5 tons. Working pressure of these two engines was 170 lbs. All had pinnace pattern marine type boilers and were coal burners. Although able to handle heavier loads than the scale model locomotives, "Ella" and "Muriel" had several disadvantages which weighed against them. To begin with, they burnt four times as much coal as the others did coke. Their limit in length, coupled with the equal overhang at either end, caused them ("Ella" in particular) to "nose" at even moderate speeds. Finally, from the driver's point of view the degree of comfort offered was nil. The writer well remembers old John Lister, soaked to the skin, on the footplate of "Ella" on a wild and rainy day. How he must have longed for the comparative comfort of the covered cab of "Nab Ghyll" or "Devon"! However, the Heywood tanks did useful work for several years, particularly "Muriel," whose steaming qualities were improved by reducing the diameter of her cylinders to 5⅝ ins.

By 1920 the traffic on the R.& E.R. was still expanding and "Sans Pareil" and "Colossus" were in need of assistance to handle the holiday crowds that flocked to Eskdale to see "Laal Ratty" at work. The new engine provided was another "Pacific," built in 1919 by Hunt & Company of Bournemouth and named "Sir Aubrey Brocklebank." The latter differed from "Colossus" only in the following respects. Steam pressure was raised to 180 lbs. and weight, in working order, to 3 tons 3 cwt. In order to allow the driver to sit lower down and thus get some protection from the cab, "Sir Aubrey Brocklebank" was fitted with a six- instead of an eight-

Closely based on the Bassett-Lowke "Little Giant" class but with a slightly larger boiler
SIR AUBREY BROCKLEBANK was the only locomotive ever built by Hunt & Co. of Bournemouth.
Within the limitations of the scale design it was a highly successful locomotive.
Photograph: Collection W. H. Whitworth.

wheeled tender. Heating surface was 12,034 sq. ins. This locomotive was 18 ft. 2 ins. long over buffers and stood 3 ft. 10 ins. to the top of her chimney.

It will be noted that "Sir Aubrey Brocklebank" slightly exceeded the limit of the British loading gauge, whereas "Colossus" was built strictly to scale throughout. "Sir Aubrey" can be said to have been constructed to the Continental standard.

It became evident in the early 1920's that a more efficient and satisfactory type of goods engine than those of the "Heywood" design was required. To this end, therefore, designs were forthcoming from Mr. Greenley for "River Esk," built by Messrs. Davey Paxman & Company of Colchester in 1923. Believed to be the first 2-8-2 tender engine on any British railway, "River Esk" was also unique in being the first locomotive in this country to be fitted with Lentz poppet valve gear.

Above and below: RIVER ESK in two earlier forms than she is today. The upper view shows the locomotive as originally built by Davey Paxman of Colchester in 1923 with Lentz poppet valve gear. She was modified in 1927 with outside valve gear and a Poultney articulated powered tender, see below.
Neither version was particularly successful and she was again rebuilt in June 1931 with a conventional bogie tender, the Poultney chassis ultimately forming the basis of a new locomotive, taking the old name, RIVER MITE in 1964.
Upper – Photograph: Collection A. Neale. Lower – Postcard: R. & E.R. Historical Series No. 8.

In her original form "River Esk" had two cylinders 5¼ x 8½ ins., driving wheels 17½ ins. dia. and leading and trailing wheels 12 ins. dia. Her total heating surface of 18,680 sq. ins. was made up as follows: tubes, 14,640 ins.; firebox, 2,540 ins. and superheater 1,500 ins. Grate area was 688 sq. ins., working pressure 180 lbs., and tractive effort 2,100 lbs. "River Esk" weighed nearly 6 tons and was 23 ft. long and 3 ft. 2 ins. wide.

Although a very successful locomotive, it was decided to reconstruct "River Esk" in 1927. The Yorkshire Engine Company Limited of Sheffield did the job and incorporated the Poultney Articulated System. At the same time Walshaerts valve gear was substituted for the poppet variety. A second pair of cylinders with a diameter of 3⅞ ins. was designed to fit under the tender and act as a booster, and the original pair were increased to a diameter of 5⅞ ins. The wheel notation of "River Esk" thus became 2-8-2+0-8-0. However, the booster arrangements did not prove entirely successful and was later removed, an eight-wheeled double bogie tender mounting being substituted.

In her present form "River Esk" has a tractive effort of 3,248 lbs. Her working pressure remains at 180 lbs. and her weight is 4 tons 13 cwt., or 6 tons 18 cwt. complete with tender. Coupled wheelbase is 5 ft. and total wheelbase of engine and tender 20 ft. 5¼ ins. Her length between tube plates is 6 ft. 7 ins. and her length over buffers 25 ft. 1¼ ins. The water capacity of the tender is 300 gallons, and the latter also holds 2½ cwt. of coke.

In 1927 considerable changes occurred in the locomotive stud. After over 10 years of hard work, "Sans Pareil," "Colossus" and "Sir Aubrey" were wearing out, and the two remaining

The original RIVER MITE combined parts from SANS PAREIL (scrapped 1926), COLOSSUS and SIR AUBREY BROCKLEBANK (both scrapped late 1927). Both of the six coupled chassis were used to make another articulated locomotive, seen above, when new, on the turntable at Ravenglass. I.C.L. No. 2, a rebuild of the Heywood loco ELLA, RIVER IRT and RIVER ESK are also present. Photograph: Collection W. H. Whitworth.

"Heywood sisters" were in similar case. Furthermore, it had been proved that the petrol-driven "rail-motors," which are described later in this chapter, were quite adequate to deal with the limited winter traffic and thus enable the steam engines to be "rested" during the non-tourist season.

"Sans Pareil" was scrapped in 1926 and "Colossus" and "Sir Aubrey" towards the end of 1927. At the same time it was decided that certain portions of all these three locomotives could be utilised to build a new locomotive in another form. The frames of "Colossus" and "Sir Aubrey" were in fairly good conditions and so were a number of other parts from all three engines. As a result, work commenced on the construction in the R. & E. shops at Ravenglass of another articulated locomotive with the wheel notation of 4-6-0 + 0-6-4. The two frames of "Colossus" and "Sir Aubrey" were reconditioned and the rear portion of each, with the trailing wheels, discarded. After selecting the best bogie and driving wheels from the three engines, they were assembled into the frames with other parts in good condition.

The Yorkshire Engineering Company supplied a new boiler with sufficient evaporative surface to supply the requirements of the four simple cylinders. The boiler and tender were then attached together by two side frames, bolted on to the sides of the tender, and on to a saddle under the centre of the boiler barrel. This saddle held a rigid pin around which the engine was pivoted. For the tender, a similar rigid pin was attached to a plate across the middle of the tender and bolted to the bottom. Two saddle plates were also bolted across each engine frame. One, over the centre driving wheels, had a hole for the pin attached to the saddle plate under the boiler. The other was fitted over the cylinders to carry the front end of the boiler and smoke-box. A plate under the latter allowed it to slide. The rear cylinders had a similar fitting for the same purpose.

Another view of the first RIVER MITE, a 4-6-0 + 0-6-4 powered tender design.
She was a powerful locomotive and originally saw considerable use on both passenger and stone traffic
before frame stresses forced withdrawal in 1937.
Photograph: Collection A. Neale.

RIVER IRT has always been the reliable workhorse of the R. & E.R. Despite her appearance she is essentially the Heywood 0-8-0T MURIEL in a new guise. Note the contrast between the Heywood 16 lb per yard rail on cast iron sleepers and the heavier flatbottom rail spiked to timber sleepers on the running line in the foreground. Photograph: Collection A. Neale.

The exhaust from the front cylinders escaped up the chimney in the normal way while that from the rear unit went into a feed water heater mounted on the rear of the tender. The steam from the boiler was conducted to the cylinders by means of flexible jointed pipes. Metallic tubing was used for the exhaust of the rear unit to the feed water heater. The new engine was completed on April 9th, 1928, and named "River Mite." Her working pressure was 180 lbs..

Having continued to give trouble, the pinnace type boiler of "Muriel" was discarded in 1927, chiefly on account of tube-plate defects. In replacement, a locomotive type boiler, of very robust design, was built and delivered by the Yorkshire Engineering Company. The rear portion of "Muriel's" frames were then extended by 2 ft. 6 ins. to carry the firebox and boiler end, and a pair of 10¼ in. dia. trailing wheels fitted into the extension below the ashpan. "Muriel" thus became an 0-8-2. At the same time, a 300 gallon tender, which also carried 4 cwts. of coke and ran on three axles with 11½ in. dia. wheels, was built for "Muriel." This tender has 2 in. dia. axles and phosphor-bronze axleboxes. In her new form she received the name "River Irt." The following are the main dimensions of this engine as she exists today:—

Boiler, inside dia., 1 ft. 8½ ins.; length between tube plates, 7 ft.; height from rail to centre of boiler, 3 ft. 0 ½ ins. The 95 sq. ft. of heating surface (4 ft. more than in her original form) is made up of firebox, 18 ft.; grate, 3 ft; and tubes, 74 ft. "River Irt" has a working pressure of 180 lbs. and weighs 4 tons 5 cwts. without tender, and 6 tons 5 cwts. with tender.

Some little time before the war, "River Mite" was withdrawn from service the mounting of the boiler not proving too satisfactory in operation. The outbreak of the war has so far prevented further modifications to be carried out on this unique rebuild of the three original scale models of the R.& E.R. "River Esk" and "River Irt" have been thoroughly overhauled and are back on the job once again as they were prior to 1939.

CHAPTER FIVE

THE PETROL LOCOMOTIVES

The 'Crewe' tractor was essentially a Ford Model 'T' car on a railway chassis. Even the steering wheel was retained. Riding on it utterly unprotected must have been awful in winter and a cab was soon fitted. Photograph: Mary Fair.

IT has already been stated earlier in this book that the meagre winter passenger traffic handled by the R.& E.R. did not justify the expense of running steam locomotives, except perhaps on Thursdays (Whitehaven Market Day) and Saturdays. On the other hand there was the Post Office Mail Contract to fulfil six days a week. It was therefore decided in 1922 to provide some kind of light-weight petrol-driven vehicle which would be capable of hauling a single covered carriage to convey the few passengers using the line between October and April. Motor-bus competition had not then made itself felt to any degree.

I.C.L. No. 1 was built by Theakston's of London and delivered in 1923. This somewhat amazing contraption consisted of a "Model T" Ford engine and chassis, all complete except for wheels. The latter were replaced by chain sprockets. The whole car chassis was bolted on to a four-wheeled frame to run on the metals and which was coupled to the sprockets by driving chains. I.C.L. No. 1 was not very successful and was scrapped in 1925.

Meanwhile a smaller machine had also been built. It was more in the nature of a petrol "scooter" and in appearance bore no resemblance to I.C.L. No. 1. The power unit was a Douglas two-cylinder 8 h.p. engine originally intended to drive a 1914 W.D. Lighting Plant.

The body of the "scooter" was of teak and a gearbox was made from that taken out of the "Model T" Ford and attached to the crankshaft of the Douglas engine. In service the latter proved to have insufficient power, so the engine out of I.C.L. No. 1 was transferred to it in 1925, when the latter was scrapped.

In 1928 the "scooter" was damaged when in collision with I.C.L. No. 2 at Muncaster Mill. The body was then rebuilt to its present form and a plate fitted bearing the inscription "I.C.L. No. 1, 1927." Although rarely used today, I.C.L. No. 1 is still in working order and her "Model T" engine is still functioning.

I.C.L. No. 2 rose, Phoenix-like, from the ashes of "Ella" when the latter was scrapped in 1926. Construction began on January 10th, 1927. A Lanchester car chassis, complete with engine and radiator, was purchased and together with the engine frame and wheels of "Ella," formed the basis of the design. The Lanchester car chassis was sawn off behind the "wick carburettor" (mounted on the petrol tank) and bolted on to two wooden baulks 6 ft. x 8 ins. x 4 ins. and attached to the locomotive frame by angle brackets. At the same time the frame was extended at either end to carry leading and trailing bogie wheels 10¼ ins. dia. The frame extensions were 2 ft. in length and carried buffer beams of channel iron, faced with oak. With "Ella's" driving wheels, I.C.L. No. 2 had the wheel notation of 2-6-2.

The 'Douglas' scooter built at Ravenglass around 1922 was the second such machine on the line and was used on light winter trains being scrapped in 1925. It is seen here at Eskdale Green.
Photograph: Mary Fair.

A Parson's Marine direct reverse gear was fitted to the gearbox attached to the engine and a universal joint was put in between it and the worm drive which was taken out of the Lanchester chassis. This worm drive had a ratio of 9·34 to 1. The differential gear was removed and a solid shaft, with a centre boss, fitted. This boss carried the worm wheel which was bolted on to it. The ends of this shaft were tapered and extended to either side of the frames to be in line with the webs of the drivers. The rear driving wheels were equipped with sprockets instead of crank webs and the crank was then fitted into the sprocket. On the tapered ends of the worm shaft sprockets were mounted, having 22 teeth to take a chain of 1·75 in. pitch. The sprockets were driven on to the tapers and hammered up with nuts. All drivers were coupled up by rods, the last driver being coupled to the worm drive by chain. Engine cooling was assisted by a water tank with a small pump to assist circulation.

The body of I.C.L. No. 2 was built of teak and all windows with brass frames and made to open. Through Parson's direct reverse, speeds were the same in either direction, although the Lanchester gearbox, with its three forward speed and reverse, was retained. This locomotive was withdrawn from service before the war.

To supplement the work of hauling the unbroken stone from Beckfoot Quarry to Murthwaite, the first of three Fordson tractor locomotives was purchased in 1926; two more were obtained the following year. These units were built by The Muir-Hill Service Equipment

Built in April-May 1927 "The Scott" was so named as it consisted of a Scott Squirrel two stroke engine on a home made frame. Capable of up to 30 m.p.h. it had a short but very exciting life before being scrapped in 1930.
Photograph: Mary Fair.

Pre-war view of one of the Muir Hill "Fordson" petrol locos shunting Theakston built stone wagons at Beckfoot quarry.

Ltd., Trafford Park, Manchester. The power unit is a standard Fordson tractor engine of 20 h.p., having four cylinders 4 ins. x 5 ins. The engine drives to a two-speed gearbox made by Muir-Hill and with the aid of reverse gear the same speed can be obtained in both directions. The final drive is by roller chain and sprockets on to the driving wheels. The wheel notation is 0-4-0[1] and both axles are coupled by a roller chain, 1·75 ins. x ·75 ins. The driving wheels, which are of cast steel, at 17½ ins. dia. and shrunk on to axles 3½ ins. dia. The latter run in axle-boxes adapted for a double roller bearing packed up with grease.

Brakes are applied to all four wheels and are hand-operated. The engine, radiator and fuel tanks (capacity 17½ gallons) are Fordson products, while Muir-Hill built the gearbox, chassis and the remainder of the locomotive. These units have proved very successful and although their normal load from Beckfoot to Murthwaite is 16 wagons, they frequently cope with 20 trucks quite comfortably. Their chassis is built up from heavy castings braced by channels and angles on top and underneath.

After the withdrawal of I.C.L. No. 2, it was decided to convert the oldest Muir-Hill locomotive to a passenger type. The chassis was therefore extended to the rear and a four-wheeled bogie placed under the extension to overcome the tendency of these tractor engines to "pitch." Thus this unit became an 0-4-4 "tank." At the same time the gear lever controls were extended and made to work from front to back, instead of from side to side. A horizontal hand screw was made and installed in place of the standard vertical hand screw brake, and the

1. *Although referred to as 0-4-0 wheel arrangement the more precise term '4w' (to denote driving wheels coupled other than by side rods) has been used in the photograph captions.*

The Muir Hill 4wPM rebuilt with a trailing bogie and 'steam outline' bodywork circa 1933 became a most useful member of the locomotive fleet, regularly used on passenger trains and stone traffic during WW2. It is shown being turned on the table at Ravenglass on 25th May 1951. Photograph: Brian Hilton.

throttle, air and ignition controls were boxed together in one unit near the brake. The throttle was made into a dual control for either hand or foot operation. A smaller fuel tank is fitted on this tractor owing to the confined space inside the bodywork. When the railway re-opened for passenger traffic in the summer of 1946, this locomotive ran most of the trains and did remarkably well. It is painted and lined out in the standard green livery and is illustrated above. No works number is carried by the oldest tractor, but the two purchased in 1927 bear the numbers NG.39 and NG.41.

Note: Whilst the original text has been left unaltered it should be noted that some of the information is incorrect. There were actually three 'scooters' at various times, not one alone. I.C.L. No. 1 was actually built by the R. & E.R. itself in autumn 1925, incorporating some parts from its predecessor, a conversion in 1923 by Francis Theakston Ltd., of a WW1 60 cm. 'Crewe Tractor' petrol loco. For a full account of the R. & E.R. early petrol and diesel locos see THE NARROW GAUGE No. 35 pages 18 to 37 (Journal of the Narrow Gauge Railway Society).

CHAPTER SIX
THE ROLLING STOCK

At the close of the working day passenger stock was marshalled in Ravenglass Station.
Photographed on 25th May 1951.
Photograph: Brian Hilton.

WHEN Narrow Gauge Railways took over the R.& E.R. in 1915 the bulk of the passenger rolling stock was of the open four-wheeled type and supplied by Bassett-Lowke of Northampton. Each coach seated eight persons, sitting two abreast. They were usually run in "sets," the end coach of each having a glass "back screen" mounted in a wooden frame. Initially, a number of these coaches were fitted with vacuum brakes, but these were discarded later. They had Buck-eye couplings, and had previously been in service on the model railways at Rhyl and Geneva.

In addition to the above stock, "Laal Ratty" acquired a number of eight-wheeled bogie covered coaches which were designed by Sir Arthur Heywood and came from the Duffield Bank and Eaton Hall Railways. Each seated 12 persons, plus two additional ones outside at either end. These were used on wet days and for the winter services. There were also some open eight-wheelers of Heywood build and on which design the later R.& E.R. open coaches, built at Ravenglass, are based. Finally, there were two other Heywood "oddities," which were more or less regarded as "show pieces." One was a bogie sleeping car and the other a Dynameter car (a four-wheeler). The latter was later converted into an ordinary closed coach and generally ran on the short winter mail train. There was also an eight-wheeled bogie luggage van, with sliding doors, which came from the Sand Hutton Light Railway and was also a Heywood product.

From 1929 onwards a steady re-building and re-equipping of the passenger stock was carried out and the present numbering scheme was commenced. The latter indicates the number of each unit and the year of construction, beginning in 1929. Thus the stock numbers commence with 1/29 and go up to 6/29, this being the total number of units built during that year. The next batch were constructed in 1932, and are numbered 1/32 to 4/32.

Nos. 1/29-6/29 were built by a local joiner. They are eight-wheelers and the first of this type put in traffic. They have light teak frames and the bogies have 12 in. dia. wheels and axles 1 ¾ ins. dia. The couplings are of the "flapper" type and bolted on to the wooden frames. These, and the subsequent ones described hereafter, are all 24-seaters, 16 ft. long x 3 ft. 9 ins. wide. All coaches built after 1929 were constructed by the R. & E. Company in their own workshops.

In 1932 Nos. 1/32 to 4/32 were put in traffic. Compared with the first batch they had heavier side frames of Columbian pine and were generally sturdier. No. 1/32 has a leading bogie with a cast iron frame and trailing bogie of the built-up tender type. Wheels are 14 ins. dia. (leading) and 10¼ ins. (trailing). Axle diameters are 1¾ ins. In No. 2/32 both bogies are of wooden construction with 14 in. dia. wheels and axles 1⅝ ins. dia. The same dimensions apply to No. 3/32, but both bogies are of cast iron. No. 4/32 has leading bogies, with 10¼ in. dia. wheels and 1½ in. dia. axles, of the built-up tender type. The trailing bogies are of cast iron and the wheel diameters are 10 ins., the axles being unaltered. All these bogies were taken from the motley collection of old Heywood stock which was withdrawn from service. Further bogies came from the same source when an additional four coaches were built in 1933. These bogies were overhauled and if found in good shape were incorporated in the new stock. Since the Heywood units were such a "mixed bag," this accounts for the variety of bogies used by the existing coaches. In spite of this it was decided to make a start in 1933 towards a standardisation of bogies used in the passenger stock. Thus coach No. 1/33 is carried on two bogies of a simple and sturdy design, built in the Ravenglass shops. These have the standard axle-box and horn-block, with 2 in. axles, as used in the freight wagons. So far they have stood up to their work quite well. The wheels are 11½ ins. dia. and are of steel, but a shade on the light side for heavy running. These wheels were taken out of some eight-wheeled freight wagons which were designed to carry 6 tons of crushed granite from Murthwaite to Ravenglass; they are described later in this chapter. All the coaches built in 1933 were similar to the previous batch, but the frames are of pitch pine which makes them heavier than the 1932 lot.

No. 2/33 has a leading bogie with a cast iron frame, wheels 14 ins. dia. and axles 1½ ins. dia. The trailing bogie is the same but the wheels are 11½ ins. dia. No. 3/33 is similar to 1/33. No. 4/33 has wooden bogies taken from one of the old Heywood coaches. All the 1933 batch are fitted with spring box couplings. Only two coaches were built in 1934 and these have pitch pine frames and tender type bogies; they are numbered 1/34 and 2/34. Tender type bogies were again used for the two additional units constructed in 1935. Both have pitch pine frames. No. 1/35 has 10½ in. dia. wheels and 1½ in. dia. axles. No. 2/35 has the wheel diameter increased to 12 ins. and the axles to 1¾ ins. Today (1947) the passenger rolling stock comprises 32 units of which 18 are of the type described above and the balance four-wheelers of the Bassett-Lowke type.

Turning to the goods vehicles, we find that these have been gradually standardised. When the N.G.R. took over in 1915, the quarry at Beckfoot had not commenced operations, and the traffic handled was mainly coal, coke, cattle cake and general merchandise up the Dale and in the reverse direction pit props and sawn timber from Irton Road to Ravenglass. A number of 1 ton open trucks were assembled at Ravenglass shops from partly finished parts They were all convertible to single bolster timber wagons. A number of the frames and axles were from Duffield Bank and Eaton Hall Railways. There were also one or two special low sided four-wheeled wagons for carrying passengers' heavy luggage, and one was invariably attached to the

A train of loaded Theakston 4w wagons approaching Ravenglass in 1951.
Photograph: Brian Hilton.

passenger trains. There was also one 3-ton bogie wagon which came from either Eaton Hall or Duffield Bank and was built by Heywood.

When the Crushing Plant at Murthwaite was opened in 1923, six 2-ton all-steel hopper wagons and 18 flap-sided 1 ton steel and wood wagons were obtained to deal with the stone traffic. Theakstons of London supplied a number of steel tippler trucks to use in conjunction with the "somersault" unloading ramp at Ravenglass.

In 1927 six specially designed eight-wheeled bogie wagons, with a stonecarrying capacity of 6 tons were supplied by the Yorkshire Engineering Company. They worked between Murthwaite and Ravenglass only and conveyed granite which had been broken up and graded at the Murthwaite Crusher. The bottom of these wagons was made like a grid. Over this grid another moving plate with similar openings in it was made to slide over the bottom. By sliding this moving grid, broken stone could be released through the wagon bottom straight into the main line trucks which were run in under the high-level ramp at Ravenglass. This enabled the tippling gear to be abandoned. In order to reduce the travel of the moving plates, they were made in two halves and were operated from the middle of the wagons by a right- and left-hand screw and toggle. These large capacity wagons were a great success, although they were inclined to "run hot" on occasions. This trouble was later remedied by equipping them with 2-in. axles and phosphor-bronze boxes.

With the opening of the "broad gauge" section from Ravenglass to Murthwaite in 1929, these tonners became redundant and in 1930 they were sold to the Romney Hythe & Dymchurch Railway for ballast wagons. In 1931 the R.& E.R. bought the bogies of these wagons back from the R.H. & D.R. They were then cut up and the wheels and horn-blocks used to make up a number of wooden wagons with removable bodies for the stone traffic between Beckfoot Quarry and Murthwaite. These steel wheels, however, proved too light for this duty and were eventually used for the coach bogies of Nos. 1/33, 3/33, and later units.

The complete passenger and goods stock of the R.& E.R. today (1947) comprises 32 coaches and 104 wagons.

CHAPTER SEVEN
THE WAR YEARS AND THE FUTURE

An interesting view of the Kerr Stuart standard gauge diesel shunting in the sidings at Ravenglass
with a rake of loaded Theakston wagons in the foreground, 14th September 1950.
Photograph: H. C. Casserley.

WHEN the World War broke out in September, 1939, "Laal Ratty" was nearing the end of another successful passenger carrying season. From then until Whitsuntide, 1946, the passenger service was suspended. Stone traffic continued unabated throughout the period of hostilities. But, in addition to this, the R.& E.R. made a modest, but most valuable contribution to the war effort of the country. Military authorities were anxious to find some suitable target for trying out certain new and powerful explosives, and it was ascertained that Beckfoot granite was one of the hardest in the country. The comparative inaccessibility of the Eskdale valley was another point in favour of Beckfoot Quarry being selected to try out the effects of these explosives. Tests were carried out from time to time during the war and yielded valuable data which in turn, led to the perfection of a number of new missiles.

Throughout the war, the steam locomotives were laid up, and when it was decided to resume the passenger traffic in the summer of 1946, the fuel shortage prohibited their regular use. The conversion of one of the Muir-Hill petrol locomotives described in Chapter Five was therefore carried out, and this little unit did yeoman service in the carrying of over 20,000 passengers in the first post-war working season. Meantime, "River Esk" and "River Irt" have been thoroughly overhauled and will soon be back again in regular service. "River Mite," owing to certain disadvantages in operation which have not yet been overcome, is not running at present.

Looking ahead the outlook for "Laal Ratty" seems a bright one. Here is a miniature railway, with all the fascination for both young and old alike inherent in such a line, which not only runs through some of the loveliest scenery in the country but also carries a steady volume of all-the-year-round mineral traffic. Long may this little railway continue to carry the holiday crowds up and down the Dale and also keep the wheels of the Murthwaite Crusher turning faster than before.

The mixed gauge (4 ft. 8½ ins. & 15in.) track at Muncaster, 25th May 1951.
Photograph: Brian Hilton.

R.& E.R.
STEAM LOCOMOTIVES

Name	Built	Maker	Type	Remarks
"Sans Pareil"	1912	Bassett-Lowke	4-4-2	Scrapped 1927. Parts used to build "River Mite".
"Colossus"	1914	Ditto	4-6-2	Formerly "John Anthony" Parts also used to build "River Mite".
"Sir Aubrey Brocklebank"	1919	Hunt & Co.	4-6-2	Parts used to build "River Mite".
"Katie"	1896	Heywood	0-4-0T	Ex-Eaton Hall Railway. sold to Fairbourne Rly, 1923.*
"Ella"	1881	Ditto	0-6-0T	Scrapped 1926. Frames used for I.C.L No. 2 (see below).
"Muriel"	1894	Ditto	0-8-0T	Rebuilt as 0-8-2 in 1927.
"River Esk"	1923	Davey Paxman & Co.	2-8-2	Temporarily rebuilt as 2-8-2+ 0-8-0 by Yorkshire Engine Co., 1927.
"River Mite"	1927	R.& E.R.	4-6-0 0-6-4	Constructed from parts of "Sans Pareil", Colossus"and "Sir Aubrey Brocklebank".
"River Irt"	1928	Ditto	0-8-2	Rebuilt with new boiler from 0-8-0T "Muriel".

PETROL LOCOMOTIVES

Number	Built	Maker	Type	Remarks
"Model T"	1922	Theakston	4-wheel	Scrapped 1925
I.C.L. No. 1	1925	R.& E.R.	Ditto	Rebuilt (new body), 1927.
I.C.L. No. 2	1927	Ditto	2-6-2	"Ella" frames used. Scrapped 1930.
Fordson No. 1	1926	Muir-Hill	0-4-4	Converted from 0-4-0 for Passenger duty.
Fordson No. 2	1927	Ditto	0-4-0	Works No. NG. 39.
Fordson No. 3	1927	Ditto	Ditto	Works No. NG. 41.
Diesel	1929	Kerr, Stuart	Ditto	4 ft. 8½ in. gauge.

The above table is reproduced just as it was printed in the first edition (apart from corrected spelling of loco names). There are also factual errors and these are corrected elsewhere in the text. The Kerr Stuart diesel for instance was actually 6w.

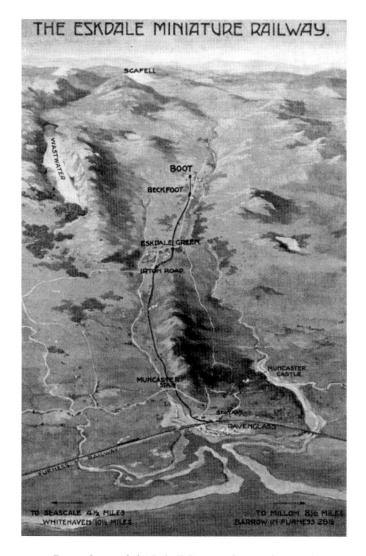

THE ESKDALE MINIATURE RAILWAY.

*Postcard map of the R. & E.R., one of a set of six cards
published in December 1915 by the Locomotive Publishing Co. Ltd.*

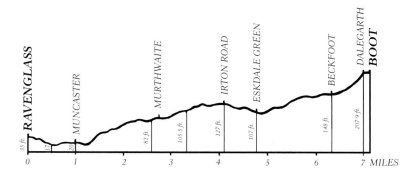

STATION LAYOUTS IN 1922

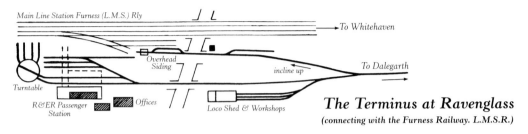

Main Line Station Furness (L.M.S.) Rly

→ To Whitehaven

Overhead Siding

incline up

To Dalegarth

Turntable

R&ER Passenger Station

Offices

Loco Shed & Workshops

The Terminus at Ravenglass
(connecting with the Furness Railway. L.M.S.R.)

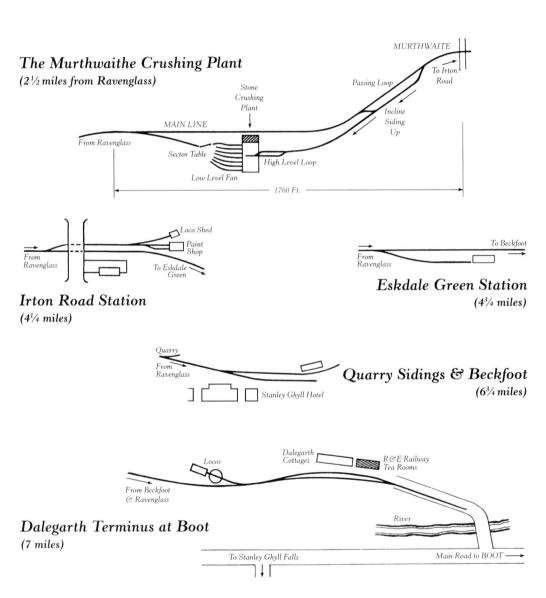

The Murthwaithe Crushing Plant
(2½ miles from Ravenglass)

MURTHWAITE

To Irton Road

Passing Loop

Stone Crushing Plant

Incline Siding Up

MAIN LINE

From Ravenglass

Sector Table

High Level Loop

Low Level Fan

1760 Ft.

Loco Shed

Paint Shop

From Ravenglass

To Eskdale Green

Irton Road Station
(4¼ miles)

To Beckfoot

From Ravenglass

Eskdale Green Station
(4¾ miles)

Quarry

From Ravenglass

Stanley Ghyll Hotel

Quarry Sidings & Beckfoot
(6¾ miles)

Locos

Dalegarth Cottages

R&E Railway Tea Rooms

From Beckfoot & Ravenglass

River

Dalegarth Terminus at Boot
(7 miles)

To Stanley Ghyll Falls

Main Road to BOOT →

STATION LAYOUTS IN 1947

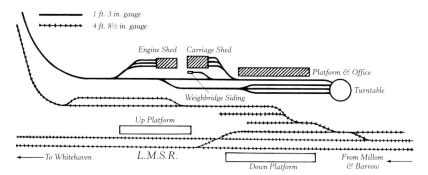

1 ft. 3 in. gauge
4 ft. 8½ in. gauge

Engine Shed   Carriage Shed

Platform & Office

Weighbridge Siding

Turntable

Up Platform

← To Whitehaven   L.M.S.R.

Down Platform

From Millom & Barrow ←

Ravenglass

Ravenglass →←

Engine Shed

Eskdale Green →

Irton Road

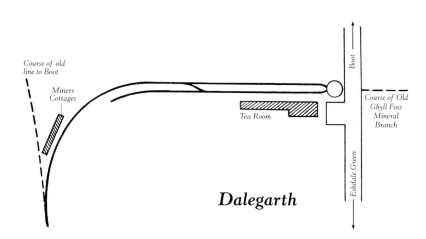

Course of old line to Boot

Miners Cottages

Tea Room

Boot

Course of Old Ghyll Foss Mineral Branch

Eskdale Green

Dalegarth